Awakening Words for the Poetically Correct

Angelee Coleman Grider

M.O.R.E. Publishers CO
Memphis, TN

Awakening Words for the Poetically Correct
Angelee Coleman Grider

M.O.R.E. Publishers (St. Louis, MO 63138, 2002-2016)
M.O.R.E. Publishers (Memphis, TN 38116, 2012 -)

For royalty fees contact the Copyright Clearance Center, M.O.R.E. Publishers – c/o www.morepublishers.biz or e-mail MOREPublishersCO@AOL.com

Angelee Coleman Grider
Editor

Edwin Marcellus T. Grider
Editor

Christopher Earl Grider
Editorial Consultant

Barry C. Wilkins, artist (inside cover)

Printed in the United States
ISBN 0-9758549-0-9   ISBN 978-0-9758549-0-7
978-1530538300 (1530538300 paperback, CreateSpace.com)

ISBN 978-1-945344-08-4 Revised Edition

Preface

Awakening Words for the Poetically Correct

Before the rain was the harvest.

Yet the planting preceded the harvest.

Even then was the anticipation –

The remote identity of an idea

that started the pain of labor, that created the thought, that led to the seed

"…and then the rain," which evoked Awakening Words.

 I can't think of a more appropriate time to tell everyone why I wrote the book. Just recently, I had a conversation with someone who had had surgery. The mood was somber, angered, resentful, hurt, disillusioned and down-right made at the world. In correspondence with the patient, I felt that no one knew why I write. If that person only understood, the statement made would not have been "I just don't trust anyone right now. I did everything for everyone, and now when I need help where are they?

 Of course, I did not hesitate to say that I was always offering to help, but for some weird reason, the trust factor was not there. The hesitation also was not there for me to say, "I'll still help you!"

 However, even in my comforting moment – wanting to reach out, I thought, I never told anyone why I wrote the poetry book. I never said that I did not bother to carefully edit it. That didn't matter. I was not about to be "politically correct" to soothe other

3

people's whims of desire for correctness. I felt hurt, ashamed, bitter, lonely, betrayed, happy sometimes, but most of all on many occasions I felt only loved by God. So, I wrote.

It took a while to create the words into motion for printing because that was not the initial thought. I was in pain. I thought if I executed a plan of relief, I could certainly feel better. It worked. Therefore, you now have AWAKENING WORDS... you now know how I felt for many years until God came to my rescue and delivered me from the pain. That's the message I leave with you – don't hurt anyone else. Just write. Hold on to pain no longer. Anger will kill you without a gun, knife or suicide. You are worth more than gold. Live a freer life.

Introduction

The book of poetry contains more painful memories than joyous ones. The ones that are crazy, are the ones most cherished because that's the inner beauty of the soul.

You may laugh when the trial and test have been completed, the pain and hurt have no longer been a reality, and through it all you've endured to the end. What does one do while "going, going through"? One pays the price, suffers, endures, and with all thy inner feelings; write it down to get it out of the mind and soul.

The pain is the reason for the magazine series in which I wrote "Poetry For The Soul". Then eventually the book came. People must realize that unless the soul is inevitably free, the body and the mind are prisoners of "stuff". When you write from the soul, freedom reaches the hearts of others who are captives, and the messages set their bodies free.

The book came enveloped because after 30 years, the idea was nourished.

Earlier works were not truly wasted.

My soul was released and after the soul was released, the cleansing came from the love of God holding on to me when I thought I would not make creative things materialize.

Being very quiet as a child, I elected to choose comforting words. Yet the inside screamed otherwise. I now tell people, "Don't ask me, if you don't want the truth".

Thus, by way of straightforward ideas, Awakening Words for the Poetically Correct was a title given by the Holy Ghost. So, if you don't want to know the real feelings I've had about life, give this book to a person with a strong constitution for realism.

After reading, you will walk away not taking a stand opposing those who open up and let out the fear, hate and anger.

I just got tired of people saying that I had not gone through any trials that were too hard for me to carry alone. God said it was also okay to let all of you know that I have had pain, but the Bible teaches us as in fasting, to let the world know nothing, for people will use confidential information against us.

Therefore, I endured until it was time to let go, write, and complete this book of poetry for my sons' sake. For God loved them enough to not let even them know that I was in a spiritual pain until God healed my body, then my mind.

I Am A Rose.

About the Author

Angelee Coleman Grider

I am a former teacher with the Fayette County (Tennessee) Board of Education at Fayette-Ware Middle School, and the St. Louis Board of Education. After 29 years, no one believed that I was serious about leaving such a fun-loving, lucrative paying job. I told them. I meant it, and I left.

I had already started my spiritually-led position as Editor of the Scale Magazine (M.O.R.E. Publisher Corp. publication), and of course I was the founder and the Executive Director of the St. Louis Writing and Performing Guild Inc. Then after 24 years of having just the name only, my sons and I incorporated M.O.R.E. Publishers Corp.

It was a shock to me to do so, but God had commissioned me long before the name originated. You see, I am a graduate of Bainesville Elementary in (Cayce, Mississippi) and Henry High School (Byhalia, Mississippi). While studying hard, I learned to read excellently by well-taught Southern teachers.

I attended Lane College (Jackson, Tennessee) and Ball State University (Muncie, Indiana). In both colleges and university, I earned degrees in English, Music, and Magazine Journalism. Therefore, I had a diverse background that was necessary to make it in the publishing business.

Insight

*A former teacher with the Fayette County School District, Somerville, Tennessee

*A former teacher with the St. Louis Board of Education, St. Louis City

*Founder and editor of the Scale Magazine (www.TheScaleMagazine.MagCloud.com) and TheScaleMagazineOnLine.com

*Founder and editor of M.O.R.E. Publishers Corp.

*Founder and Executive Director of the St. Louis Writing and Performing Guild Inc.

*Founder and editor of Stir Up The Gift – Focus On "U" TV (UPN46 TV) and "We've Got Stories" (ION TV 50-1) and "We Got Stories" (YOUTUBE and LiveStream.com)

*Founder of the VGReaders Club

*Founder of the First St. Louis Independent Writers and Publishers Conference

*Radio and TV Program Producer (on Live365.com and on ION TV 50-1); WKRA

*Alpha Kappa Alpha Sorority, Lane College (Jackson, Tennessee)

*Kappa Tau Alpha Journalism Honor Society, Ball State University (Muncie, Indiana)

*Grant writer

*Bainesville Elementary (Cayce, Mississippi)

*Henry High School (Byhalia, Mississippi)

*Primerica Financial Services

*International Society of Poets

*Suited-Up Ltd. Founder (SHC Adult Health and Day Center)

*Who's Who Among Professionals

*National Storytellers Network Member

*Mississippi Burial Insurance Agent

*St. Louis Publishers Association Member (1996)

*Author and Publisher

*Notary Public

"Dedication"

THE MANUSCRIPT IS DEDICATED

"To God" who showed me the best times of my career; who planted the pain inside of me to bring out the nurturing of love through the will-power of writing and brought forth the blossom when He poured the rain and harvested the Awakening Words.

To my Mom,
Songwriter, poet, and author of Black Treasure in Mississippi and
The Best of Revival Times, A Music Book, and Greener Pastures
Mrs. Florence Virginia Wilkins Coleman

SPECIAL THANKS...

My sons for wishing me well to do what I wanted to do, not taking from my life, but adding joy.

My brother, Rev. George W. Coleman Jr. (PhD) for wanting me to stand alone.

To my friends and Arkansas in-laws who were always waiting for a call though knowing God had already commissioned me to do other things, but you loved me anyway.

To Denise Hairston
George Hairston
Fannie, Dennis and Count Lebby who were like my sisters and brothers.

To my aunts (Della, Mary, Nina, and Earye) who were my first writers when I said I had a dream.

To my uncles for the faith:
Herman, Aaron Jr., Jeme and Cleveland

Contents

Affiliations

M.O.R.E. Publishers CO   http://www.morepublishers.biz

SUITED-UP Ltd.

Stir Up The Gift Enterprise   StirUpTheGiftEnterprise.com

The Scale Magazine LLC   www.TheScaleMagazine.MagCloud.com

StirUpTheGiftTV.com

Gifted1der Media Productions

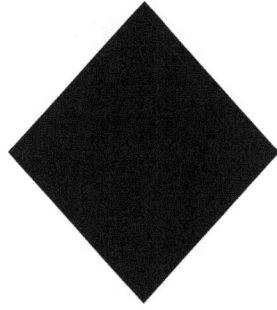

Poetry for the Soul

Poetry Contents

Poetry Contents

White As Rice

All About Me

Is That What Life Is All About?

Freedom

Oh God

Beauty

Mansion In The Sky

I Don't Have To Cry No More

The Ins

I Remember

The Christmas Bell

Loneliness Less Than Happiness

Whole

I Believe

I Dreamed

I Am My Mother's Child

The Eagle

Wessing   Console

Poetry Contents

Poetry Contents

———

The Harvest

Inside Is The Harvest.

◆

"Inside Is The Harvest"

Inside is the Harvest.

◆

"HARVEST"

After the harvest and then the rain

After the low and then the pain

After the riches of the earthly man

Then you will walk in the fold of His hand.

After the peace of the sadly beast

Jesus shall come and restore the sleep,

And rest from the world that so sorely retains

The wretch of the world that caused too much pain,

Rest from the wearing and tearing of my soul

Into a world that has made all whole.

"I'm Ok"

I'm Ok. I think of things that have driven us apart,

and I think of the dream that I had in my heart.

But now that, that dream I can no longer see,

I'll be happy with my new love until eternity.

Life

Life is like a ball game with on-lookers, pitchers, and players.

The on-lookers are those beside you;

The pitchers, the competitors you must face.

The players are you and others trying to exist in this race.

You work hard every day trying to reach a goal or make a good play;

yet knowing success is easy if you could only make third base.

Saying, "I know then that I can get home safely."

But listen,
there are those players who you certainly must watch –

the ones who throw curve balls grasping for your failure by trying to get you out.

For then the game is theirs with the cheers, the boos, and the shouts.

"THE NOISE"

The noise, the noise, the noise…

My ears are amidst a thousand sounds
and I can't hear.

I write but I can't speak.

The multitude is too large.
It's an entrapment and I can't be free.

I scream yet I can't be heard,
for the noise has overpowered me.
I'm lost in sound.

Priest's cloth – Public Domain Photo

"ORDAINED"

You were born with a silver spoon in your mouth.

John said it.

You were born to blaspheme my savior.

But the resurrection has not come.

For within, you know He is still the truth and the light.

When it appears, you will know that the resurrection has come.

"FAMILY TREE"

One day I searched
my family tree.

As a mirror, it revealed
only brother and me.

However, something gave me a
curiosity quest.

I knew I had to put my mind to rest!

Not afraid of anything I might find,
I looked a little farther back in time.

Being young, some things I didn't understand.
I had to grow to know life on this land.

I was once reared in a world of two,

"But listen", the tree said.
"There's more than brother and you.
Don't falter! But love, infinitely and carefree."

Suddenly a vision appeared so unmistakably clear.

Like father, she was somewhat a stranger, yet sweet and dear.

Yes.
One day I searched my family tree.

Surprisingly,

I found not two,   but three.

(Photo by Angelee Coleman Grider)

27

"BE YOUR OWN MAN"

Be a giant.

Reign in victory!

Go! Go! Young man.

Be proud.

Stand tall.

Be your own man.

PublicDomainPictures.net   Resurrection Cross

"SAVE"

Save Jesus Christ,

the one and only Savior of all men.

Save Him – for the
slaughter of evil men,
persecutors, and sinners.

"Love, Joy, Peace"

"LOVE"

Love,   Joy,   Peace

All three, from me, you can't have.

They're within.
Those are inner beings.
God gave them to me.
I can't give them to you, but all three are definitely free.

Love, joy and happiness –

I changed my mind about peace,
for if I have the latter two, the peace will not cease.

I still can't give them to you, for they are some things you must find.

However, if you remember that I love you, you can wait until it's time.

Wait until you have the joy that brought you peace within
and understand why I couldn't give them to you,
even though I always loved you as a friend.

Waiting

Waiting is a state of for-ever-ness not knowing how, when, or if an end will ever come.

You just sit looking for the worst,
but hoping for the best.

There is a feeling that you can either take it or leave it.

You're always hoping that you'll be able to keep your head up high and accept whatever comes.

Who is He?

"WHO IS HE?"

More like a ball

More like a gem

Less like a string

Less like them

Only one person - Unique in his cause

A myth?

A dream?

Whatever, he's Santa Claus.

A Welcomed Friend

It takes more than an idea to start the ball rolling.

Yet, you know that something has to come,

something that is the answer to all of your dreams:

A prayer,

a hope,

a miracle answered.

No matter what it is,

it's a welcomed friend.

If

If only the sky stayed full of stars,

If only the world was full of love,

What a great life this would be, to live in peace 'til eternity.

I can imagine the pain endured
by forefathers who fought for freedom and brotherhood.

Yet I earnestly pray and hope for the rest
that God will someday upon me bless.

Though hearts be heavy and burdens not light,
there is a dream that I can dream each night.

It starts with a battle fought by men,

and ends with a solution –

Peace, Amen.

Am I Getting Old?

"Am I Getting Old?"

TIME can tell.

He stumped his toe.

Public Domain Photo – PXHere.com

He turned around.
He winked his eye.
He fell to the ground.
Snow fell on him.
The wind blew cold.

"My God," he said, "Am I getting that old?"

Still

Still just as
yesterday
            a tear may be a smile.

Although the steps get
   shorter,
           a walk will still be a mile.

        Yet when it's time to ponder
     of those years so quietly gone by,
we look upon the younger in the image of still
          a little child.

Still the youth do climb
   that rugged growing hill
and today will always be yesterday's
tomorrow as the world keeps turning
still.

**Two generations – Still
building legacies**

The Storm

"AND SO IT BEGAN"

And so it began.

10:44 was the time and was God pleased?

I arrived, sleep-awakened by the thunderstorm as the newscast blasted the moment of discerns.

I appeared to cry, and God said, "Write".

Tell the story.

Show of God's glory!

Was He pleased?

It stormed.

It rained.

Heard by all throughout was the voice of the one who ordered us to war. "The only way to remedy this is the war." He said it. "War. War. War."

The night before spring, in a promised new day, God said to me, "Go. You must live until you die. You must live until you die."

God told us "Live!"

Yet was the storm a sign?

I Thought of You

The door cracked.

The wind blew, and I thought of you.

The well became a reservoir for eyelids full of tears as memories flashed before my eyes of happy yesteryears.

I laughed at all the corny jokes.

I listened to long, tall tales.

I always listened for the phone to ring and I jumped each time you came.

Lest I forget the pain, the sorrow, the care you've shown always;

Lest I forget the melody you carried in each and every way;

Lest I forget, for when the door cracked, I thought of you today.

I Am Climbing A High Mountain

There is a mountain before me and I am afraid to climb.

Leadership –

That's what you told me.

Fierce may be the road; hills and valleys too,
yet some earthquakes flatten out earth's roads.

Time only knows when,
but God knows the crown was on mine – a head of wisdom;
an arm of protection
and a safety net for the angered to see through me,
to come to know the God that is ever on the throne.

"Listen To The Drummer"

"Listen To The Drummer!"

A band here, a band there – Listen to the drummer.

A word is spoken in an undertone – Listen to the drummer, the base for all harmony in which all relations thrive; upon which all relationships are built.

Listen to the drummer for He only speaks once in a loud tone – then silence.

He says it no more for the brass cymbal overtones his voice.

Hurt, pained, sometimes - He thought he was disillusioned.

He dared to say what did fill his heart.
He dared to say it.

Listen to the drummer, a silent tone once the band begins to play.

Friends, lovers, wives, listen to the drummer.

"...And God Called Another Moses"

I sat asking, "What would God say?"

I suddenly became afraid, for God said, "Tell her I called".

"Who Lord?"
"My church. I meant to call her Moses!"

"Why Lord?"
"Because Moses stands for strength.
The church has called my people of multi-colors: Strong people of torture.
They endured the whips of slavery.
They fought the Civil War.
They will lead my people of belief in Jesus Christ.
They will withstand the millennium.
They will meet me, and I shall call them Moses."

"When Lord?"

"This day. The bush burns. The Pharaohs come. The Hitlers are no longer in
exile. The Veil of the temple has been mended. And my people have been
called."

"Moses," God requested of His church, "Lead my people to Gethsemane,
through the shadow of the crown, over the banks of Jordan. Then come up to
higher plains of War."

I sat down again.

I asked, "What would God say?"

...And He said, "Tell them I called. For they are one faith, one church (my
church).
When they ask, 'Where are the patriarchs?' Tell them, 'Fret not.'"
So, the people of the church God has called you to be another Moses.

"I Have A Bee"

"I Have A Bee In My Mailbox" (Copyright 2002)

I have a bee in my mailbox!

That's all that I could see,

was a great, big, old, black bumblebee 'a coming after me.

Public Domain Photo

He came straightforward,
in spite of the bright, blue skies.

Yes, all that I could see was that he looked me right between the eyes.

I fanned him with my little fan of mail I had so scarcely caught,

but believe me, my bundle of mail was the last thing in my thoughts.

Yes, I have a bee in my mailbox, or so it may seem.

To me it really doesn't matter where he came from;
I just let out a scream.

He flung his wings so vibrantly with a charge not so merry to my heart,
and I could only think of the fight I wish that I did not start.

Yes, it's my entire fault, even if he came from out of that tree.

The only thing that matters now, is that he's running after me.

From This Day Forth

Photo by Angelee Grider

From this day forth you will be blessed by God above.

From this day forth He will be cherishing your love.

Can't you hear His prayer spreading throughout the air,

"From this - from this day forth"?

Instrumentally, I bought eyesight:

two rims, a frame and the light.

Yet, I couldn't see the light though I knew it had come.

It was the time of love,

for He caressed me just as I was about to fall and from this day forth,

I knew He was mine, and I was His.

"White As Rice"

White as rice, is all I can see whenever someone tries to disrespect me.

I reflect on the cotton fields,
the buttons,
and the boughs on the hills,
and in the valleys,
and in the streams flowing below.

I can still think of the times when I was so mad because Papa had to tote
sacks that made him all so sad.

The times made him sad
to wonder what it would be like to
be
a better friend
and to stand
face to face with that of what others called a white man.

All About Me

When I remember January with a dew so worn and grown,
I think of the 29th of December on that early, frosty morn.

I think of all the crying of babies yet unborn,
and I think of all the crying when the baby girl had come.

She had come with such a pretty smile that cheers your tears away.

Yet she came with an everlasting song that sings until this day.

She came with such wedding vows that no bridegroom could resist;
yet somewhere along the way her pretty smile did grow amiss
for wedding gifts that were for her moved oh so ever so.

But wait!
Through the obstacles of pain and despair,
she still smiles and thanks dear Jesus,
for that crying is still there.

Still there to remind her of that lovely winter morn,
is the thought that Jesus, too, was born upon just yarn.

Is This What Life Is All About?

Is This What Life Is All About?

Love,
Dreams and undaunted Wisdom?

In that case, I just must enjoy it!

Manual labor is what we complain about, but God gets the glory.

Our strength surpasses who we are
and any honor we can hope to obtain.

Fragility backs down with just a muster of concern.

I go on winning as I go.

Freedom

Freedom is like a blue bird so lively and free:

Beautiful

Sensational

Painless

Wonderful

Magnificent

Thought to be unbearable

Yet turned out pretty darn good

Wonderful

A way of life that you thought you never could claim,

Reframe or know.

Yet freedom is a something of which you don't want to let go.

Oh God, I Can't Believe This Is Happening Again

OH GOD, I CAN'T BELIEVE THIS IS HAPPENING AGAIN:
RAIN,
SUNSHINE,
ALL IN ONE DAY'S TIME.

It happened just this Friday:
Two days ago

Pulled right from under me

Whisked away listlessly

No fight. No argument. Just gone.

Then again, I got the phone call:
More news than bad.

It was the same call.

Come and get it if you want it on your terms I can't keep calling.

This time it's only a warning.

I'll fight back if I have to.

This can't keep happening to me.

What do you want?

To destroy my every timeline?

You bastard!

You got my soul at the whim of nothing to save one other.

You can't have me this time.

God prevails only when you are caught.

I think it's your turn, and not mine.

You're sure to die first, not me.

Do it again to me and I'll last forever.

Remember that Jesus did.

"MORE"

More precious than gold is
He who surrencompasses the love of Christ,
embedded down within the soul.

Grappling to hold on, for life's summer breeze remains a fading image
of life sustaining only limitlessly probing,
taking, scheming, devastating.

The life vanishes.

Yet more precious than gold is he who holds
steadfastly to the love of Christ in his soul.

"Pays"

"PAYS"

If I pay on acceptance,
I'll forget to go back to Indiana and north for Ohio.

I'll forget to stumble when I fall in my tracks,

and I'll forget that I no longer paid you back.

Poetry for the Soul

I Remember Washington

I remember Washington

Lilacs,

Rubies,

Steps

and Tulips

(It was spring; you know).

Tight cars, two movie stars

Stair steps, more baggier bums,

Bright lights, slammed doors,

Barred stores, White House woes –

I remember Washington.

A Thought For The Season

As the Christmas season rolls around,

don't forget that Santa's back in town.

Polish your smiles and your silverware too,

and remember that, this time of the

year, friends are many, not few.

Maybe

Had this world not been created,

Had man been only stone,

Had all not been created,

Then God would have been alone.

A Cross

"A CROSS"

A cross – Bloodstained

Blasphemed

Iniquitously labeled

Blasphemed
For me.

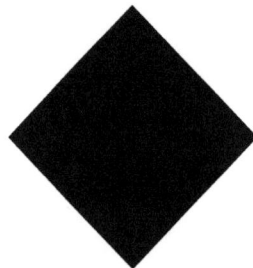

Wandering

The gold is the color of my rainbow for it is the symbol of my ring –
The ring I wear so true to show love.

It represents the everlasting, endless ray
that says tomorrow will never come;
It will always be Today.

Today I smiled.
Tomorrow I'll frown.
Yesterday I cried.
For "now" is all I have.

Yet, say no more, for tomorrow is my day!
I'll dance.
I'll sing.
I'll laugh.
I'll cry.

But happy I'll never be.

Long, short
Long, short
The hands of time.

Sing, sing, sing.
Laugh, laugh, laugh.
Go forth and be reborn –
Reborn with a crisp newness like the early dew of morn.

Go forth and fly to the outer depths of reality.

It is love.

Hate makes you want to live for eternity.
 What is love?

It is a phone call in the midday and hearing someone say, "I love you."

It is a caress at midnight and a whisper where reality no longer exists.

There is only the fantasy of love and joy,

A world of vision of multitude and thanksgiving…
A vision of rapture and fortitude.

Proclaim and rejoice in gladness for true love is everlasting -

NOT Wandering!

WHAT IS EVANGELISM?

(Prose)

As I walked, directions came across my mind.

Am I an evangelist?

Am I a missionary?

Am I me just doing the "work of the Lord"?

Then I remembered the sermon from Sunday's pastor in the pulpit.
This is what he said.
"It's good to be here. It's good to be anywhere and be able to tell about it."

So, I thought, regardless of what I am, my appearance should tell others
that I am happy that God has left me alive.

Then he asked, "How can you have an annual day to celebrate what you've done
and have not done anything all year?"

So, my answer was, "Whatever I call myself, be sure I have the works to back me
up".

Have I evangelized?

Have I commissioned others as hopeful candidates for Christ?

Am I satisfied with what I'm doing to give God the glory, so I can also be "I Am"?

"BY THE WAY, I THOUGHT I SAW YOUR DADDY TODAY"

His hair was balding, with just a touch of gray.

Yes, he saw your mother, but we both tried not to see,
for the agony and the rage just kept on pulling at me.

I know we shouldn't talk about certain things for God
has given us more wisdom than pay, but son, as I
said, I thought I saw your Daddy today.

You are a fine man, my son – freckles all deep and wide.
Amazing how you look like me, yet you take from the other side.

When you're no longer a young man and as grown as grown can be,
I hope we'll still look alike and your spirit will be like mine –
warmer, caring, and concerned about others' pride and joy;
a spitting image of me, one day, I pray.

But son, I think I told you; I thought I saw your daddy today.
6 feet. That's what you tell me.
Oh, my how you've grown; rebellious in nature too, as you assert your very own.

Eyes brown like the shadow, to make any woman proud.
Soft-spoken and mystical looking to make a jealous woman tired.

Intelligentsia, they call you and I'm happy that you're a son of mine,
but when you frowned today, there was an image I did not want to see,
and I had prayed, never to find.

Yes, today was different, in every sort of way.
And oh, by the way son, did I tell you, through your image,

I thought I saw your Daddy today.

A Dream

"A DREAM"

Quickly as a fleeting ship,
it came in the night –
More beautiful than a sunrise at dawn.
It came in a vision so bright and clear:
Fast, clear, then vanished to be no more.
In a moment of silence, my dream was gone.

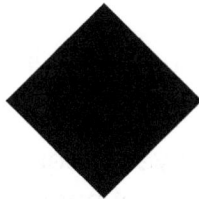

"GRANDMA'S HANDS"

(Written in memory of my Grandmother, Mama Ora "Sweet" Moody Wilkins)

She left me one morning when she knew I was on the phone.
She couldn't call to tell me that God had called her on.

She only spoke to my mother who had begun to cry, and the only thing mom
could say was, "Mama Ora told me to tell you she tried."

"She tried to tell you through her senility days that she would be safely gone - the
day when you wouldn't know that God had called her home.

You just didn't want to listen because you loved her so,
but way down deep inside, you knew that God had told you long ago."

"He told you about the sugar cookies, and sweet potato pies
but you weren't ready to listen because she was right before your eyes."

Yes, Mama's gone on to glory and it will be to my surprise that I'll get there to
see her in a mansion in the sky.

Yes, I do remember that Sunday before Christmas morn
that my mother called to tell me
that Grandmother was leaving then and going on home.

I asked the Lord, "Why couldn't she wait for me to come and sit by her side?"

He replied, "She's tired child, and she asked if she could rest her hands and
close her eyes".

Even though senility took her many years before she was ready to go,
I realize that it was a sign from God that her chapter was about to close.

He let me be there with her for many happy days, and the last that I remember is
she said that she read her Bible and prayed.

The Road To Success

The road to success is not straight.

There is a curve called Failure,
a loop called Confusion,
speed bumps called Friends,
red lights called Enemies;
and caution lights called Family.

Your flats will be Jobs.
But, if you have a spare called Determination,
an engine called Perseverance,
insurance called Faith,
and a driver called Jesus,
you will make it to a place called Success!

Be of good courage.
Be of good strength.
Be not afraid.

Meditate and be pain free.

Make thy way prosperous.

Be a success!

Mansion In The Sky

(Lyrics)

There is a mansion
on a hilltop
in the sky,
Lord, in the sky.

Christ who's King of kings,
answers problems from above,
Before the sky,
Yes, before the sky.

See, I'm going home one day
when my Lord says,
"In the sky,
child, in the sky."

I will be ready
to go with the Lord,
In the sky,
yes, in the sky.

Written in honor of my father Elder George Willie Coleman Sr. of Oakland, California, for his home going, November 10, 2003

"I DON'T HAVE TO CRY NO MORE"

(Lyrics)

I don't have to cry no more.
I don't have to cry no more.
He paid the price.
He made the sacrifice and I don't have to cry no more.

I don't have to moan no more.
I don't have to moan no more.
He paid the price.
He made the sacrifice and I don't have to cry no more.

I don't have to cry no more.
I don't have to cry no more.
He's coming back again, taking me in His wings,
and I don't have to cry no more.

Refrain:
Jesus,
you are my all and all
and I don't have to cry no more.

Jesus,
you hear me when I call,
and I don't have to cry no more.

I don't have to cry no more.
I don't have to cry no more.
He's coming back again, taking me in His wings,
and I don't have to cry no more.

I don't have to cry no more.
I don't have to cry no more.
He's coming back again, taking me in His wings,
and I don't have to cry no more.

Beauty Is In Seeing A Rainbow

Beauty is in the rainbow that my Mama showed me one day,

High up in the sky when the rain had gone away.

The water smelled of fresh blooms;

the cotton sack smelled of hay,

but in spite of it all

I had found favor that day.

I didn't know what was up there,

beyond the clouds that I could see,

but I knew that two people were special to God –

and they were Mama and me.

Beauty is in seeing a rainbow.

ACG

"THE INs"

The ins and outs - When do you go?
Where?
How?
Why?

Yet foreclosure can't come!
You told me so, by now.

That's it!
Then is now!

Now you got to go.
To the top!
Get going!
It can't wait!
That's it.

Will you ever be that long?
Entrepreneurial,
Entrepreneurship,
Entrepreneuring
That's all.

Anything, but nothing.
No more waiting.
Got to grow now!

That's all. NOW!

"Loneliness Less Than Happiness"
(Inspiration)

Loneliness is like a bottomless pit.
The hurt goes on, and on, and on...

Happiness is knowing that you are special to someone.
It is being loved and giving love in return.

It is a flower in full bloom at the dawn of morning.
It is a sweet cup of coffee and a jellyroll.

It is caring and respect.
It is sharing and giving.
It is love. love. love.

Happiness is hope that makes you want to live for eternity.
It is a phone call in the midday and hearing someone say, "I love you."

It is a caress at midnight and a whisper of rapture that says,
"I want to be close to you."

It is loneliness that is filled with the pain of need.
It is being cherished.

It is warmth on a cold winter's night.

It is a word of inspiration when hope is overcome by pity and fear.

It is fear being replaced by encouragement.

It is a raindrop that cools the heat of the sun.

It is the smile that inspires when all other seem lost.

It is a breeze in high humidity.

Yes, happiness is this and more.
 It is whatever makes you smile instead of frown,

feel up instead of down,

wanted instead of being rejected,

loved instead of hated,

being needed instead of being lonely.

Happiness is only a state of mind.

                    Loneliness Less Than Happiness

"THERE'S AN ANGEL IN HEAVEN"

(lyrics)

Dedicated to the Griffith Elementary Youth in Ferguson, Missouri who died in 2002 after being struck by a car in front of his school.

There's an Angel in Heaven of whom we all love.

There's an Angel in Heaven who is looking from above.

There's an Angel in Heaven of whom we all know.

There's an Angel in Heaven for God told me so.

I Believe

I dreamed but I lost the flavor.

My hearing became that of the unknown.

Yet I lived.

I believe I was born.

"WHOLE"

I am whole for the faith that I kept through my tithes;

Whole for I let No unsaved die.

I am whole for the harvest of Jesus' coming day;

Whole for I labored until the final pay.

I am whole for I now sit not wronged by the world,

but I labor each day in the Father's, the Son's, and the Holy Spirit's faith.

I Am My Mother's Child

"I Am My Mother's Child."

(daughter – look-a like)

Brighter than an envelope
so shaped to a "T",
that's all I never wanted,
but I wanted her to be like me.

Brighter than a rainbow,
I stand here so loud.

That's all I ever wanted
was for my Momma,
of me
to be so proud.

.

Just like an image of things as they be –
regardless of what I wanted,
my Momma is just like me.

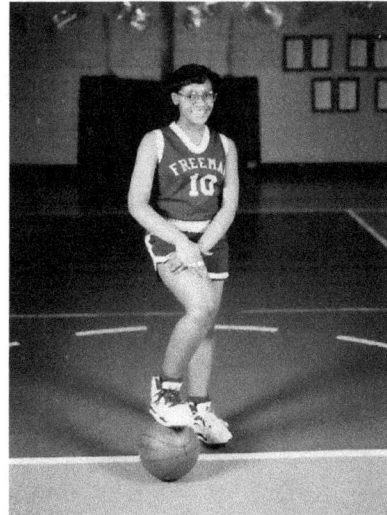

(Mother as a child)

73

PublicDomainPictures.net

The Eagle

There's an eagle that flies in midday air
who soars over plains from east to west.

But when his wings grow tired from the flight,
even he goes home for his rest.

Wessing

"WESSING"
Wessing was what Wessing is –
A theme of my imagination:
cajoling,
simple,
less smoother than I remember,
A sad note of faith,
not believing,
vanishing.

Wessing is what Wessing does.

Wessing is anything.

Copyright 1999

Console

When the cares of my heart are many,
thy consolation cheers my soul.

Be it the light that lifts the soul or the flame that burns the light,
God delivers them all into the hands of that which He may.

He raises the sunshine that brightly gleams in the sky.
He waves His hands and the thunder roars.
He bats His eyes and the lightning flashes.
He smiles and there is eternal life.

God glorifies all things to which no man can compare.
He is that He is.

"BEAUTY"

Inner being
 An inner spring

That soul of wholeness:
kind,
mild,
a sweet unperturbed madness of sanity

Kind,
loving,
caring
Meanness no more.

I had to learn to love me before I could love anyone else.
(Age 6 – during a field trip; Age 24 – left; Age 36 – right; Age 68 – below)

"LOVE IS"

Love is a shining star, so bright and clear.
Sometimes it can't be expressed but you know that it is there.

Love is like a windstorm, changing, changing and not still.
You try to hold on to it, but you know you never will.

Dream what you want,
long for what you may,
leave me forever
or by my side always stay.

"LOVE"

Love!
I don't know too much about that.

Hate – Hate had envied me so until the grass of weight could not sustain the pain of not knowing.
Hate – I got that in me because love has not taken over.

Love – I don't know too much about that.

When Love Isn't Enough

When love isn't enough,
and pain is all I have

When pain overtakes me,
and seems to forever last;

When love isn't enough,
and pain is all I have

When pain overcomes
I'll feed my soul at last.

I'll feed my soul with the anger for
the deep feeling that has gone,
when love isn't enough. (Copyright
July 20, 1998)

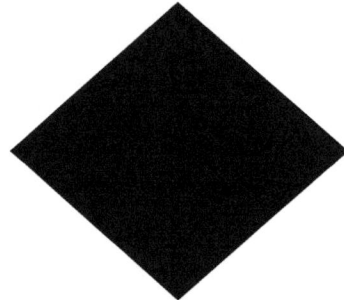

"BILLS LIKE A GEICO"

Once upon a time there were bills flying by –
So many in all pieces.
I thought that I would cry.

Then I asked my Savior,
"How could I say the magical verses like a GEICO in desert places,
and urchins
then turn around and pay all of these bills,
that I'm sure were my Master's will?

He said,
"I don't know my child.
You're already over the hill…
I told you to do my will: To promise to pay your tithes each day.
So, I guess you'll pay your bills the same as tithes –
'someday and some way.'"

So, I listened to the Master
and got my butt up off the ground
and you know,
I started to pay my bills the next time as my paycheck and my tithes came
around.

Pixnio.com Public Domain Photo

Poetry for the Soul

"THEN YOU ARE FINALLY A WOMAN"

If you can keep your head
when all around you there is crying
and the thunderous patter of little feet
or the man calling for your affection is yet trying to be discreet;
and as you walk nine months, closer to the fold
you stand up and tell the world you are bold.

If life just seems to pass you by with only your memories in its hand,
we know certainly that you're a woman, and not a man –
for men just seem to go out and find satisfaction when there is a need,
while women linger behind,
fulfilling needs of others and doing good deeds;

But when the time of flourishing comes to receive all awards,
there will be a woman in the flock for she bore all of the stars;
yes, from within her gentle womb.

"On Love And Life"

What is love to me?

I will tell you so.

It's cherries and ice topping where the cold wind does not blow.

It's trying to get that which must be begot.
It's knowing when to go and when to move out.

Love is making believe that life is so grand.
It's more like muskmelons that are walking hand in hand.

It's more of a fragrance that's never really very loud,

but it's more that brings you together than you can understand.

So God Looks Like Me?

"So God Looks Like Me?"

Pray here.
Stay here.
Stand alone, on one.

Does my God look like me?

Turn around the analogy: four noses, four toes, and a soul so carefree.

This isn't what I look like, but does my God look like me?

A pure soul; a body whole;
too many body parts that I don't have.

Amazing!
I never could make any sense of three –

So, I must be an image of Thee!

Public Domain Photo

More Gospel Voices

More gospel voices like a silent sigh;
won't say what they're thinking;
they just go home and cry.

Babies being cradled struck;
girls being raped;
back in the hollows,
are the Gospel voices in church.

Wake up my brothers. Speak up my sisters. Let your voices arise.
Today is today and never again will this time ever be.

"Give it time," our fear says.
But just think,
today is today and don't give it away.

More Gospel voices,
O silent cries,

No moans.

He Died With A Crown

By Angelee Coleman-Grider

He Died With A Crown

Like a thief on the cross
He laid His body down,
For the world's mistakes
He wore thorns of hate,
But He died with a crown.

People cried murder.
Pure blood ran down
But with Him there on the cross
 were two, who were lost,
One had to be found.

He's the Savior of saviors
Who promises freedom unbound
In a world without race
Deplored hate and disgrace
And gifts of golden crowns.

He's a Savior of saviors
And jewel of all men
And He promised me
If I would live free
He'd come back again.

Refrain:
Yes, yes my Jesus,
He laid His body down,
And for the world's mistake
He wore thorns of hate
But He died with a crown.

He Died With A Crown

He was brutally beaten
with blood flowing down.
But with Him there on the cross were two who were lost,
and one had to be found.

Refrain:
Oh yes, my Jesus,
He laid His body down.
For the world's mistakes, He wore thorns of hate,
but He died with a crown.

Like a thief on the cross,
He laid His body down.
For the world's mistakes, He wore thorns of hate
but He died with a crown.

Oh, yes, my Jesus
He laid His body down.
For the world's mistakes, He wore thorns of hate,
but He died with a crown.

"I saw the rain soak"

I walked among the pebbles along a birch-view tree
Sullen
Quiet
Spring-like no more.

Still voices calling from beneath the earth once dusty and allured
"Water, come to me.
Raindrops fall; come to me."

The cold, wintry rain was not silent. It had fallen hard, boisterously
yet now quiet as a fragrant mist.

Not even an umbrella was required to sustain it;
total silence from above.

But the earth still called,
looking to see what could be found.

Pebbles beckoned from below.
"Hear us," they said, "as we grow, dustless."

The rain bubbled from within each pebble so clear – Bubble. Bubble. Bubble.

I could hear as I walked among the mist of rain fallen
to beckoning pebbles of the earthly ground.

I saw the rain soak.

Copyright December 24, 2002 ACG

'Cause

Rain in the sunshine,
Summer in the clouds,
My goodness,
I didn't know you were so loud.

Sprinkles of the ocean
Splatters of the sea,
If God had not owned the river where would the earth be?

Right of the Mississippi,
South of Brook-a-land,
East of Potosi,
North of Thailand,
Just a bit of snowflakes
Not a trifling bit of harm
If you don't shut your mouth, the fire-bell will alarm.

MASSIVENESS

Massiveness of parts is just like the whole of uncaring

pouring in nothingness into a wound of sore repute

and standing alone in an aisle of self-decisiveness.

The pain.
Oh, the pain.
Debts paid in full. Sharing no more.

All the cares are gone.

The God of Wisdom,

Guide them,

more on the right side as on the left.

Bed Mites

Creatures of lice, the roaches' cousins so fair –

Unbeknownst to me was the little creature there.

"Bed mites," said the angel.
"Now what should you do?"

I smashed it with my pencil,
for it was the closest thing near.

"Bed mites," I thoughtest, "running so free.

Should I be crazy to stomp around my bed
as a wild one, a lunatic, and struck the sucker dead?"

I chose the latter as my defense.

"You don't mess with me!" and struck it without a whence.

"The little creature running around my bed.
Next time I'll pray harder and then spray until you all are fed."

Marriage

Marriage is like a wild wind
that blows and changes its course in the night.

It shifts.

It sways.

It moves like a snake in the grass.

It swirls and has no straight definite path.

It is quiet, yet breezy.

It carries the force of a Storm!

It is fascinating!

Yet sad.

Who knows where the wind blows?
Who knows which way a marriage will go?

Photo by Angelee C. Grider (Mother's funeral wreath)

The Saddest Good-bye

The saddest good-bye is in departing, from the friend you've had so long.
Yet there comes a time when each must go a separate way of his own.
Yet the saddest good-bye is not in leaving but it's when you realize you're left alone.

You're left alone to cherish the memories that you have so dear
and to think of all the ups and downs that you've had through many years.

You see a friend departing.
Then there comes the drop of one sad tear.

A handkerchief is handed to wipe the tear from your eye;
and a smile comes on your face in order to hide that sad sigh.
But nothing can erase the memory of the saddest good-bye.

Many nights, as a child, I cried because he stayed in so much trouble at school and home.

Many altars, as an adult, I prayed on, for the remission of his drinking.

Yet many days I drove him to his cancer therapy sessions and I never once stopped preaching "Jesus loves you" to him.

Then many moments we got a chance to talk and, I knew that he believed for he said he wished he could have been a better dad to his children.

Repentance is what dries our tears. For it took only one day for God to let me see His glory and answers to my prayers.

You see, during our last day together, there was a halo on his shoes. He was being anointed by God. Our God called him home, and I was sad, for that night I was too tired to talk to him, and God said, "Just pray."

"I CRIED"

THE SUN DID SHINE.

THE RAIN FELL.

THE BIRDS SANG,
AND I CRIED.

94

"A Change of Heart"

There are times when I look back, into a past I once knew.
I see visions so fair and true –
Visions of a loved,
Visions of you.

My love was once strong.
Or so I thought that no brow could tear us apart.

Then came another so fair and true, and my love for you was lost.

WAR

From around the building
the young man came.

"He has a gun",
they said, as the petite
security guard
closed the door.

We froze to a command.

"There's a student with a
handgun", we were told.

Yet, if the lady behind me had kept walking and not caught my arm,
I would have not stopped.

Was I afraid?

Was I crazy?

For me, God only knows.

I couldn't leave her.
Or could I?
Was she afraid?

God knows this was our first inclination of war that was said of many days.
So why be afraid?

Is the end today or tonight?
I must have been afraid. I'm supposed to be afraid! Why can't I feel afraid?
You had been told.
It would come. And so it came.

"GO FAR"

Go far young man. Go far.

To the depths of the world, go far.

To every corner of time,
Go far. And in the end return.

Return to the place you left behind for better things
for the best is yet to come.

Return knowing that you have somewhere to return.

Return knowing that you can go home again before

"nothing is still the same."

Poetry for the Soul

"FIVE, FIVE,   FORTY-FIVE"

Five, five, forty-five
No love have I known.
Five, five, forty-five
No love have I shown.

Just For Consideration

It's hurting to be unloved. Yet it's worse to be loved, but not loving.

Same as always - Great!

"ONLY A RAINDROP"

Only a raindrop can wash a tear away.

Only a raindrop can save a dying soul's prey.

Only a raindrop can keep him whole each day –
only a raindrop,
only a raindrop.
(September 1, 1998)

"IS THERE ANYBODY OUT THERE?"

Life is too short to waste, yet too long to really enjoy.
It's a waste.
It's a ferry.
It's a star.
Whatever it is, it's there.

I walk in a daze wondering "Where am I going?"
Looking yet not seeing; Speaking yet not saying a word; Comprehending yet
not hearing.

Where am I?
I'm in a daze;
lost in my own emotions.

I can't get out.
Nothing else can get in.
Around and around in circles I go from day to day wondering Am I lost?
Am I found?
Am I no longer in existence?
Does anybody know where I am?
Does anybody know who I am?

I'm me.
Yet, I'm not myself.
I'm somewhere.
Yet I'm nowhere.
Where can I go?
Where can I hide?

I'm lost and can't be found.

Poetry for the Soul

"FAITH"

The faith that I have is the substance of things hoped for,
the evidence of things not seen:
abounding love,
a perfect spiritual soul - Faith
a glorified God,
a cherished heart - Faith
better workers for Christ,
powerful prayers - Faith
health surpassing wealth,
times of worlds not seen - Faith
reaping of harvest,
a powerful God abounding in grace,
Faith

"THE FAITH"- A labor of love,

reaping of a mind to serve God,

desiring to serve throughout all **mankind.**

Faith.

"NO PEACE"

Angelee Coleman Grider

I woke up one morning and
the birds' singing was loud.

I threw my window open and I saw not a cloud.

I shouted out, "I love you!"
but got not even an echo in return.

I turned and hid my tears and because of shame, I wanted to run.

I ran to my bedroom and the loneliness followed me there.
I ran to the world,
but not a soul was near.

I said, "Lord, I'm sinking.
My time is growing thin."

He replied, "My dear child, there is no peace within."

I looked in the mirror to reveal the problem now.
I had to find consolation, but I just didn't know how.

The mirror said, "I show only what is without.
I can't give an answer until the real you have come out."

"I Believe"

I believe that one day I'll sing, to the glory of God.

I believe that one day I will praise His name forever more.

One day, I believe, that my bones will create new bones;
that my Savior will restore me to His kingdom.

I believe, you, one day will.

"I AM"

I was a robin up in a tree.

I flew.
I fell.
I sang with glee.

I was proud.
I was bold.
I was brave.
I grew old.

Now I'm a sparrow on a swing. I lost my heart and forsook my wings.
No longer do I fly free with the wind, for I'm a dove who is lost within.

Our Saviors

I wanted to say hello, to the one who wore the
screen – brown, yellow, green, Army fatigues.

Are you even stationed here,
in this city walled by deceit and shame?
 I wanted to stay my distance, although I wanted to go.

Moving to my right, he moved along to the left side turning,
yet almost embodied in one soul so close, yet far, far, away.
I wanted to say hello.

Do you have a moment to stay?
Does your watch tell me that you
have a moment,
to talk of the situation in Tehran;
of the fire-arms that you carry;
of the desert walk in the sand?

 I wanted to say hello,
even though I surmised – He is exactly like me:
afraid, alone, but wise.

Wise to the cumbersome isle area
we tried to maneuver down
during the lonely Christmas Eve morn
in an aisle all cluttered with grocery shoppers all snuggled,
warm and cocooned;

hustling – bustling forgetting the boys, girls, men and women on the other shore
far into the harbor of foreign lands so far.

Yet, I dared not interrupt your strut for you are -

"Our Saviors"

As you tried to walk so soft, not loud
magnificently adorned in Army fatigues so proud.

I wanted to stop you for a moment,
to say hello with a smile
just to say, "I appreciate the struggle you fought in foreign isles."

CERTIFICATE IN LIEU OF LOST OR DESTROYED

Discharge

Armed Forces of the United States

This is to certify that

GEORGE W COLEMAN 34 423 880 Private First Class
170th Port Company 486th Port Battalion

was discharged from the

Army of the United States

by Honorable Discharge

on 13 December 1945

at Camp Shelby Mississippi

Given at Washington, D. C.,

WM: E.
Major
The Ad

DD FORM 303A

"HOT FUN IN THE SUMMER"

There's not a friend like Jesus in the sweltering joy of love,

the exhilarating singing, the escalating shouting –

(Hot Fun In The Summer).

High hasn't made its debut until it acclaims the need for the Word.

The Word.

"For God so loved the world that He gave His only begotten ..."

sitting, Reading, PROclaiming PULSe RISING

Adrenaline fluctuating for summer reading is good. After the reading, the rain, the winter cold, the harvest, the gain.
 Some loss and then after spring, summer comes

 Lazy, hazy days of summer that bring time for undiluted reading (of the Word)

The Word - that showers, sears, motivates and
inspires –

Hot fun in the summer!

And You Think I Have No Pain

Are we both not humans having the same eyes to see and cry?
The motivation of strife keeps us going.

The same bills…
When the gas company cuts yours, mine too!

The rent man comes the same time for dues that are due
to do that which I should have done.
    ……and you think I have no pain.

Yes, I drive right past you in a clean car that somewhat looks new,
with my head up.
That's just pride.
That's all that I have left.
    But you think I have no pain.

Who am I?
You never knew.

I'm the midnight crier.
    … the crumb collector,
    … the neat-looking façade.

Who am I?
    I'm the one next door.

    …and you think I have no pain.

"Friends"

I had some that I thought were true.

I lost one that was new.

I need one, new or old that is careful, kind, fearful, or bold.

If one you do truly find,

tell him, I too am kind.

And maybe we can share until the end, that true, long- lasting, trustworthy, faithful,

and loving relationship as….

FRIENDS

Just As Soon As My Feet Strike Zion

(lyrics)

The Finale
"Just As Soon As My Feet Strike Zion"
arr. by A. Coleman Grider

Lyrics:
I'll make it alright
Soon as my feet strike Zion

Just as soon as my feet strike Zion
Just as soon as my feet strike Zion

I'll make it alright.

Refrain:
Soon as my feet strike Zion
Just as soon as my feet strike Zion
Just as soon as my feet strike Zion
I'll make it alright.

Verse 1
Haven't been to Heaven, but I've been told,
Streets up there are paved with gold.
I'll make it alright. I'll make it alright.

Verse 2
Jordan River is chilly cold; Chills the body but not the soul.
I'll make it alright. I'll make it alright.

"Just Then"

Just then, I thought I saw you afar in the way,
but I can only see a vision of yesterday.

I thought I was seeing you in faraway lands,
but oh, I forgot, it was just then.

Just then is a long time when you can make the noise,
that glistens in your eyes and sounds like little toys.

Just then is wonderful in the arms of a man,
for you know he loves you in a moment of "just then".

Yes, We Can

(In memory of Barack Obama, USA 44th President; 1st Black President)

I can be more than I've ever wanted to be.

On "red-letter days" I paint the path beneath me red so I can see my way.

On "blue alert days" the sky turns from gold to a blue sky for flying.

During "droughts" I soar beyond the dry wind to find the cool of the day.

"Rainy days" keep me nourished and parched free.

When I'm " "weary and sad" I perch myself above the agony of the ground.

As I see the golden leaves turn green, I cherish the thought of spring.

Just as I think I'm "down and out",

I hold the thought that I've told you what's lovingly in my heart.

I bow down deep on my knees to give reverence to God,

And I say to myself "I can do all things through Christ".

Beyond that thought, I keep saying to myself,

Yes, I can!

By A. Coleman Grider, 2009

This Old House

by Angelee Coleman Grider

This old house once knew my mother.
This old house once knew my friends.
This old house holds many memories that won't be back again.
This old house
This old house
This old house is where my grandparents began.

This old house is long in standing
At Route 1, Box 12, Tenn. – 10.
This old house healed hearts and families,
that ever came within.
This old house
This old house
This old house is where my grandparents began.

Refrain: This old house – This old house
This old house holds all the memories
That won't be back again.
This old house
This old house
This old house is where my grandparents began.
                Copyright 9-20-2013

"BOXED"

BOXED
BOxed
BOXEd
BOXED

That's how I feel within –
Shut up inside.
Not even wisdom will come in.
That's how I feel this day with others standing -
others also sitting just as a riverboat rises with the water sprays eroding behind,
on the sides, and underneath.

Boxed.
Cellophane tape me.
Ship me around.
Sail me across the sea.
Stamp and send me to thy love.

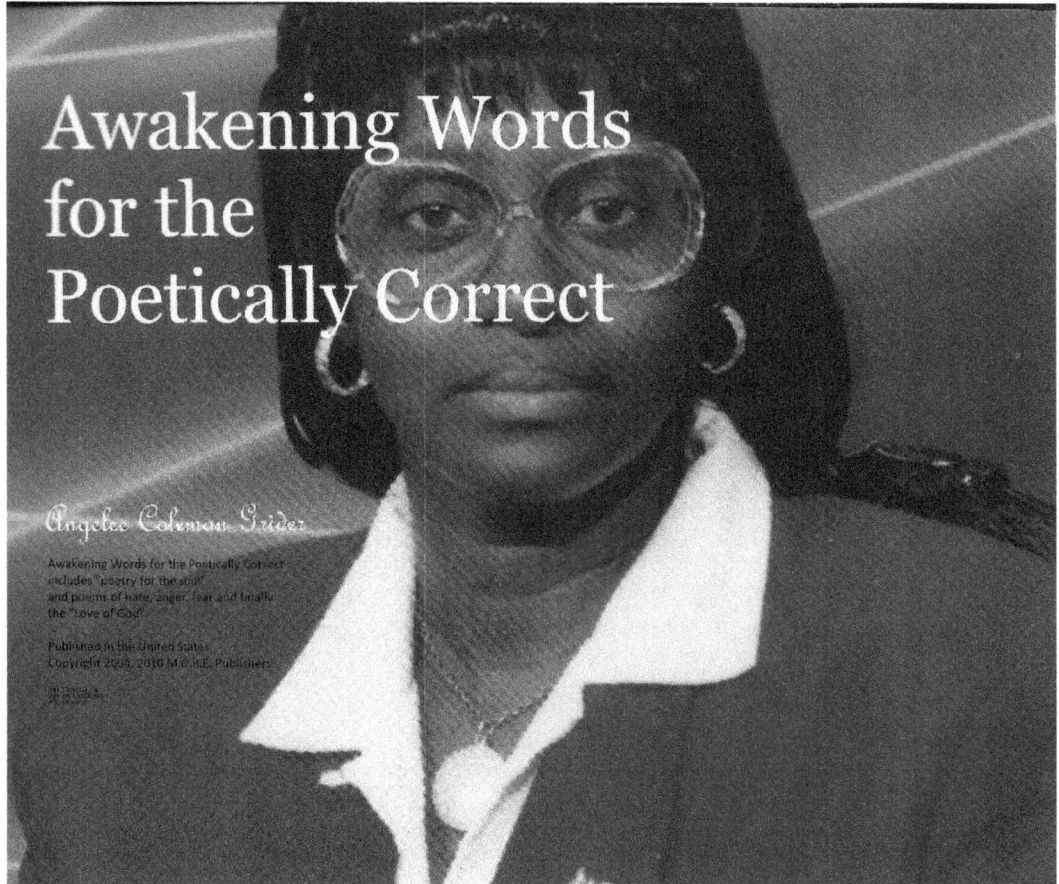

Awakening Words
for the
Poetically Correct

Angelee Coleman Grider

Awakening Words for the Poetically Correct
includes "poetry for the soul"
and poems of hate, anger, fear and finally
the "love of God"

Published in the United States
Copyright 2009, 2010 M & R.E. Publishers

Biography

Biography

Angelee Coleman Grider is a native of Cayce, Mississippi where she experienced success as a renowned child writer, and a poetic reader during community and church gatherings.

She scholastically began writing longer pieces as a junior at Lane College in Jackson, Tennessee under the auspices of Mrs. Lois Broady who recognized Miss Coleman's talent, helped her to travel and to subsequently write a play about the assassination of Martin Luther King Jr.

The play was submitted to a University of Missouri playwright contest committee. The entry was not a winning entry, but the committee advised her that her talent was wonderful and if she wanted to attend graduate school in Columbia, they would help her receive a scholarship.

Ms. Coleman Grider instead pursued a journalism master's degree at Ball State University where she was inducted into the Kappa Tau Alpha Journalism Honor Society upon the recommendation from one of the advisors, Dr. Earl Conn.

Presently, she is the founder, executive director and talent search organizer for the St. Louis Writing and Performing Guild Inc. She also, with the help of her mother, expanded the writing business to formulate M.O.R.E. Publishers Corp., a nationwide entity for beginning entrepreneurs.

She has also completed the final version of her musical CD "Mansion In The Sky".

Her earthly achievements:
High School:
Who's Who Among American High School Students, Honor Society, author and composer of the 1968 class song;
graduate of Henry High School,
Byhalia, Mississippi.

Published Works

Selected Readings
Angelee Coleman-Grider

CD available.

College:
newspaper and yearbook staff member;
alto and soprano singer in the concert traveling choir;
reporter for the Lane College campus and submitted articles to the Jackson Sun city newspaper;
Bachelor of Arts Degree with a major in English and a minor in vocal Music;
a member of the Beta Chi Chapter of Alpha Kappa Alpha Sorority.

Graduate:
Master of Arts Degree in Magazine Journalism from Ball State University in Muncie, Indiana;
inducted into the Kappa Tau Alpha Journalism Honor Society.

Professional:
Former English teacher in Fayetteville, Tennessee
and journalism teacher for the St. Louis Public Schools;
an independent representative of Primerica Financial Services,
and a member of the St. Louis Publishers Association

Published books, poems and awards:
1995 Editor's Choice Award from the National Library of Poetry;
published poetry in the Creative Review Magazine;
2001 "Opinion Shaper" editorial writer for the North County Journal;
member of the International Society of Poets;

"Who's Who for Professionals";
member of the National Notary Public Association;
published the poems:
>"I Remember",
>"The IN's",
>"I Believed That I Could Fly",
>"Boxed";

Published works:
I Have Creatures of This Land
Amazing Animals of This Land
The Scale Magazine.

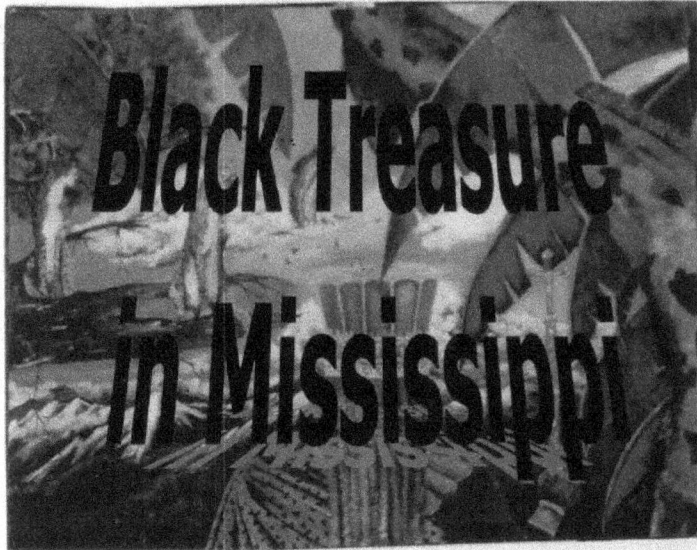

Black Treasure
In Mississippi
And The Best of Revival Songs
Revised Edition

Florence Virginia Wilkins Coleman

**Revival Songs Available on CD.
Co-authored and Produced by
Stir Up The Gift Enterprise**

I Have Creatures of This Land.

-A Book of Poetry for Children-

by Angelee Coleman Grider

Book and CD available.

MRS. DOWDY SAID...

Homespun Theology of Folk Wisdom

Angelee Grider

AMAZING

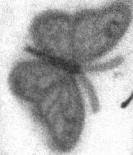

Animals
OF THIS
LAND

A Book of Poetry for Children

Angelee Coleman Grider

Family of Writers

Mother   Cousin   Author   Son

...AND GOD CALLED YOU

FLORENCE VIRGINIA WILKINS COLEMAN

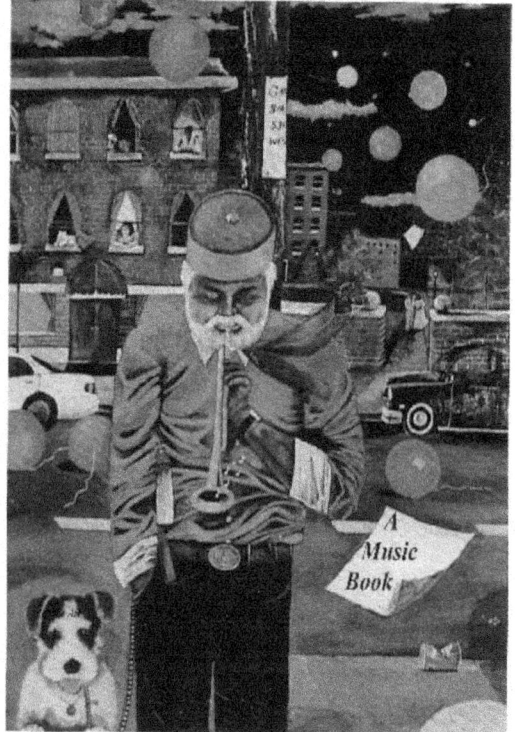

A Music Book

This Is My "Will"

How to Write Obiographical Sketches
[Your Own Obituaries]

Angelee Coleman Grider and Lizzie B. Davis

Glossary of Technical and Poetical Terms

Abbreviations –
MS = Mississippi;
MO = Missouri;
.com = communication system;
@ = at;
e-mail = electronic mail address;
Ave. = avenue;
M.O.R.E. = more of religious eloquences

Allusion – an indirect reference of one object to another object

Analogy – two objects being compared with the writer using more details.

Anecdote – a short story meant to be entertaining, usually about a personal experience.

Biography – an account of a person's life written as if a 2nd person wrote it about the author.

Cliché – a statement that has been used too many times, sometimes referred to as
"old fashioned"

Hyperbole – exaggeration used to stress a point

Quotation marks – punctuation marks used to show emphasis to be placed on certain words or used to indicate the title of poems or songs.

Rhyme – words or phrases that sound alike at the end of lines or verses

Poem – words arranged to have rhythm, rhyme and emotions when read; sometimes written in free verse with no strategic pattern; a composition in verse style.

Poetry – the writing of expressions in beautiful or "high class" thoughts and feelings in verse form

Prose – a paragraph; a composition; a speech that is not written in poetry/verse form.

Rhythm – the distinguished flow or movement felt during the reading of a passage or while singing a song; denoted
accents or beats

Royalties – money paid to the writer, by the publisher after copies of a book are sold.

Style – the way that an author writes such as with short, emphatic phrases or with long sentences

Verse –
a short subdivision of a poem, sometimes called a stanza.

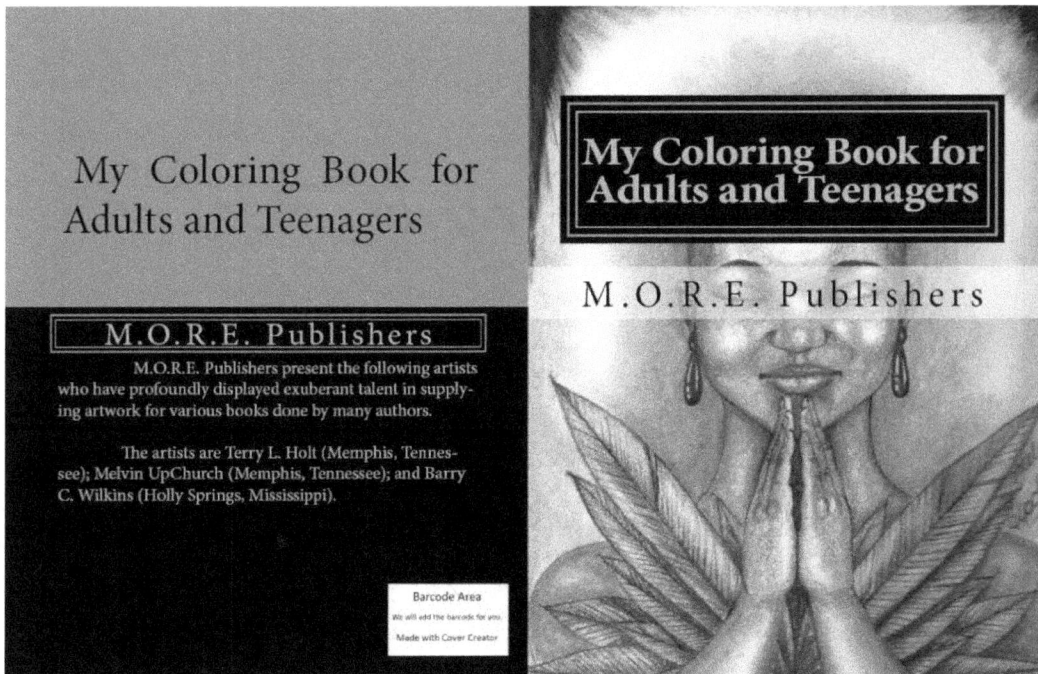

My Coloring Book for Adults and Teenagers

M.O.R.E. Publishers

M.O.R.E. Publishers present the following artists who have profoundly displayed exuberant talent in supplying artwork for various books done by many authors.

The artists are Terry L. Holt (Memphis, Tennessee); Melvin UpChurch (Memphis, Tennessee); and Barry C. Wilkins (Holly Springs, Mississippi).

Barcode Area
We will add the barcode for you.
Made with Cover Creator

My Coloring Book for Adults and Teenagers

M.O.R.E. Publishers

Wings

Songs of Praise
and Hymnals

Angelee Coleman Grider

A Few of My Favorite Things

White Wine Chicken

And

Green Beans

Ingredients:

2 tomatoes, grilled

2 packages of frozen green beans

1 chopped onion, red

1 dash of seasoned-salt, (Season to taste later.)

1 cup of water

2 tablespoon spicy Italian Vinaigrette and marinade sauce

2 tablespoon sea-salt butter

1 package white-wine chicken couscous, frozen

Grilled white meat chicken, chopped finely

Roasted zucchini and eggplant

Add more white wine, if desired. (I do not).

Instructions:

Combine ingredients in large pot.

Let set for 30 minutes in refrigerator.

Bring dish to boil.

Simmer on very low setting, 2 hours.

Cool, eat and enjoy.

Adapted by Angelee Coleman Grider

January 14, 2018

… just as a riverboat rises with the water sprays eroding behind, on
the sides,
and underneath.
Boxed.

(Excerpts from "Boxed")

Index

Meet the Staff

Angelee Coleman Grider

Editor and Publisher

MOREPublishersCO@AOL.com   https://morepublishers.biz

April 12, 1972, Mt. Pisgah CME Church (Cayce, MS)

"Marcellus T."

"Might Not Mean Much"
(The Single)

Edwin Marcellus T. Grider, Editor and Music Publisher

Gifted1der Media Productions Studio, 314-809-2481

and

CHRISTOPHER EARL GRIDER, Financial Advisor

Pictured on page 122

Rev. Madeline Coburn, The Scale Magazine CEO

Coburn Enterprise

Kevin Pulley, Media Marketing

Minister Larry Rodgers, Media Marketing

ForWord Records

Harold Hitchings, Videographer 901-268-3298
Stir Up The Gift Enterprise

"MAYBE": Had this world not been created, had man been only stone, had all not been created, then God would have been alone.

Awakening Words
For The Poetically Correct

Angelee Coleman Grider

www.ingramcontent.com/pod-product-compliance
Lightning Source LLC
Chambersburg PA
CBHW081213020426
42331CB00012B/3010